ILLUSTRATED GUIDE
TO THE
ROYAL BOTANIC GARDENS
PERADENIYA

ILLUSTRATED GUIDE TO THE ROYAL BOTANIC GARDENS PERADENIYA

H.F. MACMILLAN

GYAN

Published by

Gyan Publishing House
5, Ansari Road,
Daryaganj, New Delhi-110002
Phone: 011-47034999, 9811692060
E-mail: books@gyanbooks.com

Distribution Network
gyanbooks.com
India, USA, Canada, UK, Australia, France

ISBN : 978-81-212-3565-5 (PB)
First Published, Colombo, 1906

2nd Impression 2020
Printed at: Gyan Press, Delhi.

Illustrated Guide — TO THE . . Royal Botanic Gardens, Peradeniya,

WITH A PLAN

By H. F. MACMILLAN, F.L.S., F.R.H.S.
(Curator)

Dedicated, by permission,
TO HER EXCELLENCY LADY BLAKE.

Published by
PLÂTÉ & Co., Colombo & Nuwara-Eliya.

W. W. CURTIS, LTD., PRINTERS AND DESIGNERS, COVENTRY, ENGLAND.

Brief Historical Sketch.

J. C. Willis, Sc.D., M.A., F.L.S., *Director.*

THE Royal Botanic Gardens, Peradeniya, date their origin back to eighty-four years ago, being opened in 1821, twenty-five years after the arrival of the English in Ceylon, and six years subsequent to the final conquest of the Kandyan Kingdom. Previous to this, however, efforts were made to establish a botanic garden in the neighbourhood of Colombo, first at Slave Island by the Dutch; afterwards by the English at Paliyagoda in 1799; later at Kew, Slave Island, in 1810; and lastly at Kalutara in 1813, with Mr. W. Kerr as Superintendent. The final transfer to Peradeniya in 1821 was made under the rule of Mr. Alexander Moon, the then Superintendent. Moon was a diligent student of the Ceylon flora, and published in 1824 a "Catalogue of Ceylon Plants," in which 1,127 plants are referred to under their botanical and native names. After Moon's death, in 1825, a succession of more or less incompetent Superintendents followed, with some interruptions, until 1844, when the famous traveller, Mr. George Gardner, was appointed Superintendent. Gardner is said to have made important improvements in the condition of the Gardens during his five years of service. He died at Nuwara Eliya in 1849, and the "Gardner Monument" (page 11) has been erected in the Gardens to his memory. Gardner was succeeded in the same year by Dr. Thwaites, who, with his great acquirements and steady devotion to science, gave a world-wide reputation to the Gardens. Thwaites' term of office extended over thirty unbroken years, during which he never left the Island. He retired in 1880, and died in Kandy in 1882, his memory being appropriately perpetuated by the "Thwaites Memorial" (page 27). Succeeding Dr. Thwaites, the office of Director was held from 1880 to 1896 by Dr. Trimen, under whose energetic rule and capable management the beauty and usefulness of the Gardens were very considerably advanced. He established the Museum of Economic Botany, opened Branch Gardens at Badulla and Anuradhapura, and began the publication of his great work, "The Flora of Ceylon," which, however, was finished by Sir Joseph D. Hooker, Dr. Trimen's death occurring in October, 1896. A brass tablet has been placed in the Museum to commemorate Dr. Trimen's memory.

By the appointment in 1896 of the present Director, Dr. Willis, a new era of progress has opened up for the Gardens. From an institution with only three European officers in 1896, the Department of the Royal Botanic Gardens now employs, besides a native clerical staff, nine European officers, viz.:—*The Director* (J. C. Willis), *Entomologist* (E. E. Green), *Mycologist* (T. Petch), *Scientific Assistant* (A. M. Smith), *Chemist* (M. Kelway-Bamber), *Curator of Peradeniya Gardens* (H. F. Macmillan), *Curator of Hakgala Garden* (J. K. Nock), *Controller of Experiment Station* (Herbert Wright), and *Superintendent of Cotton Experiment Station* (C. J. C. Mee).

Besides the general extension and organisation of the Department, an excellent Laboratory for scientific research, and furnished with modern equipment, has lately been built in the Gardens, with smaller accessory laboratories at the Experiment Station and Hakgala and at Henaratgoda Gardens.

List of Superintendents and Directors from the commencement of the Gardens in Colombo, with date of appointment:—

1812—W. Kerr.
1816—A. Moon.
1825—A. Walker (Acting).
1827—J. MacRae.
1830—G. Bird (Acting).
1832—J. G. Watson.
1838—J. G. Lear (Acting).
1840—H. T. Normansell.
1843—W. C. Ondaatje (Acting).
1844—G. Gardner, F.L.S.
1849—G. H. K. Thwaites, Ph.D., F.R.S., C.M.G.
1880—H. Trimen, M.B., F.R.S.
1896—J. C. Willis, Sc.D., F.L.S.

1895—*Curator*, H. F. Macmillan, F.L.S.

Staff of the Royal Botanic Gardens, Peradeniya (1906).

Introductory.

"PERADENIYA, the most beautiful gardens in the world," "The Garden of Eden"—these and similar phrases are well-worn expressions of tourists and travellers who visit the Gardens every year to the number of about 3,000.

Peradeniya is supposed to take its name from *pera* (guava) and *deniya* (a plain), which would suggest an early connection with the introduction or cultivation of fruits, as the guava is not indigenous to Ceylon. The site was chiefly a royal demesne of the Kandyan Kings before the formation of the Gardens, evidences of this being still existent in the form of some carved stone pillars in different parts of the grounds. Peradeniya is accessible by road or railway, being about 70 miles from Colombo, and nearly four from Kandy. The Gardens are situated on the Colombo-Kandy high road, about ten minutes' walk from the Peradeniya Railway Station and Post and Telegraph Office. Close to the Gardens there is a comfortable Resthouse, capable of limited accommodation, and Kandy, the nearest town, has several good hotels. There is a good service of trains to Colombo, Kandy, Hatton, Nuwara-Eliya, etc., and most mail trains on the main line carry refreshment cars.

The Gardens are at an elevation of about 1,600 feet above sea-level. The area is nearly 150 acres, and beautifully undulated. The climate is moist, hot, and very equable, the mean annual temperature being about 76° F., though as low as 55° F. is sometimes recorded in the early mornings in January and February. Rain falls at frequent intervals, and on an average of about 170 days in the year, with a total yearly average of 89 inches. February and March are the driest, and April and May the hottest months. The vegetation is purely tropical, being characterized by an abundance of climbing plants or lianas, palms, bamboos, pandanus or screw-pines, epiphytes (orchids, ferns, etc.), and lofty trees, the latter often having buttressed roots. The leaves are generally large, thick and leathery; the flowers usually brilliant and considerable in size, and the fruits often of immense proportions and borne on the trunks of trees or older branches. Other striking tropical features are the great variety of bird, insect, and reptile life. Lizards or chameleons of diversified forms are everywhere, and snakes of numerous species abound, from the venomous cobra and repulsive polanga to the harmless, beautiful, green whip-snake, which lives mostly in trees or shrubs. With reasonable precautions. however, the snakes do not constitute an appreciable source of danger.

The following itinerary is sketched out with a view of enabling visitors to see the most in the shortest time possible. While it is not necessary to follow in detail the route described (indicated on the Map by arrows), this, on the other hand, may be extended and particulars filled in as time affords. All the main roads are open to carriages—a point of no small importance where the climate is hot and oppressive—and visitors are usually content, through want of time or other causes, with what they can see from their carriages. But it should be remembered that to really see the Garden and properly appreciate its beauty and treasures, it should be explored on foot. Most of the principal trees and plants are labelled, and there are small directing-boards at the corners of the principal drives and walks, so that with the help of this little Guide the visitor should be able to see and appreciate at least some of the attractions of Peradeniya.

I am indebted to Messrs. Plâté & Co., the well known Artist-Photographers, and Publishers of this Guide, for the photographs of the "Flying foxes on the wing" and the three portraits, to Dr. Willis for those of "Hantane View" and "Thwaites Memorial," to the Colombo Apothecaries Company for the original photograph of the "Candle Tree," and to Messrs. F. Skeen & Co. for the group of the Staff. The rest of the illustrations are selected from photographs taken by the Author.

I have also to thank Mr. W. Nock, retired Superintendent of Hakgala Gardens, for kindly paging the Index, in England.

H. F. M.

Guide to the Gardens.

APPROACHING the ENTRANCE, the grove of Assam rubber trees (*Ficus elastica*) on the left will attract attention. These form a striking feature on account of their singular flattened roots meandering over the ground like huge reptiles, but the trees are now fast decaying, being over seventy years old. This tree in its young state, with its large, glossy leaves, is the familiar "Rubber-plant" so commonly grown in pots in temperate countries. Here it grows to a height of 140 feet or more; it yields a good rubber, known commercially as "Gutta-rambong," for which it is being conserved and cultivated in Burma, etc. On the triangular grass plot outside the gates are two conspicuous trees; the taller is the "Honduras Mahogany" (*Swietenia Mahogani*), the other being the West Indian "Star Apple" (*Chrysophyllum Cainito*).

 Grove of Assam Rubber Trees

On either side of the entrance is a tall African "Oil-palm" (*Elæis Guineensis*), the principal source of commercial palm-oil, which is obtained from the seeds by boiling. Draping the gate pillars is the graceful Brazilian climber (*Bignonia unguis*) which produces in April its pretty yellow flowers in great profusion, followed by curious slender pods three to five feet long. On entering, the LODGE, where the Visitors' Book is kept, is passed on the right. Immediately in front is a magnificent oval group of palms, containing over fifty species. Among the most interesting may be noticed the straight Arecanut or "Puwak" (*Areca Catechu*), the seed of which forms part of the common masticatory of the East (the other principal ingredients being lime and the leaf of a pepper, *Piper Betle*); the Date palm of Egypt (*Phœnix dactylifera*); the Ivory-nut palm (*Phytelephas macrocarpa*), whose large seeds furnish vegetable ivory; the great "Inaja" or "Cocurito"

MAIN ENTRANCE.

MAIN CENTRAL DRIVE.

palm of Brazil (*Maxmilliana regia*); the Palmetto palm of Florida (*Sabal Palmetto*); the Great Thatch palm of Jamaica (*Sabal umbraculi fera*); the Sealing-wax palm (*Cyrtostachys renda*); the handsome *Verschaffeltia* and *Stevensonia* from Seychelles, and *Dypsis* from Madagascar. Growing under the shade of palms may be observed the "Panama-hat plant" (*Carludovica palmata*), from whose palm-like leaves the celebrated Panama hats are made, also the "Madu" or "Sago" plant of Ceylon (*Cycas circinalis*), the starchy pith and seeds of which are both articles of food.

MONUMENT ROAD.

The road should be followed to the left, round the palms, passing the Lake Road on the left. At the junction with the latter is a "Cochin-goraka" tree (*Garcinia Xanthochymus*), cultivated for ornament and for its pleasantly acid yellow fruit; behind it is a shrub of *Napoleona imperialis*, whose flowers are supposed to resemble an imperial crown. Next to this is *Amherstia nobilis*, a native of Burma, and one of the most beautiful ornamental trees of the tropics (p. 29).

Following round the Palm Group the visitor arrives in the MAIN CENTRAL DRIVE, one of the principal features of the Gardens. The drive is bordered on either side by a large and varied collection of foliage and flowering plants, gradually rising in height from edgings of "lilies" (chiefly a *Hippeastrum* with pure white flowers) in front to large shrubs behind, these being backed and shaded by tall and overhanging trees, which are mostly draped with ornamental climbers.

Continuing for a short distance the MONUMENT ROAD is passed on the left, and the LIANA DRIVE curving to the right should be followed. Notice in the corner the tall Sandbox tree of South America (*Hura crepitans*), which has peculiar explosive fruits. Round the curve on the right-hand side is *Clusia rosea*, a small West Indian tree which yields a tenacious resin from the stem, and immediately opposite is a tree of the Ceylon Satin-wood (*Chloroxylon swietenia*), one of the most beautiful of timbers.

VIEW IN OCTAGON CONSERVATORY.

The huge lianas which characterise this drive, thrown in loops and festoons from one tree to another, consist chiefly of species of *Calamus*, a climbing palm whose cable-like stems grow to several hundred feet in length; these furnish the well-known cane or rattans used in furniture-making, etc.

Coming to a small circular tank with a fountain, carriages may stop in the shade so as to afford inspection of the Flower Garden, Plant Houses, etc. Growing in the tank are interesting aquatic plants, as the Egyptian Papyrus (*Cyperus Papyrus*), the cellular stems of which, cut into thin strips and united together with Nile mud, constituted the papyrus of antiquity; the floating Water Lettuce (*Pistia Stratiotes*); the Lattice Leaf plant or Water Yam (*Ouvirandra fenestralis*); the Water Hyacinth (*Eichornia speciosa*); the clover-like fern (*Marsilea quadrifolia*); the Water Poppy (*Limno-charis*

SNAKE-LIKE CLIMBER (*Bauhinia anguina*).

Humboldtii); the Sacred Lotus (*Nymphæa Lotus*) and others. The two Assam rubber trees (*Ficus elastica*), like those at the Entrance, cannot fail to arrest attention. On the right a path passes under the singular climber (*Bauhinia anguina*) with tortuous snake-like stems. This leads to the completely shaded NUTMEG WALK, bordering upon which is the SPICE COLLECTION, including Cinnamon (*Cinnamomum zeylanicum*), Allspice (*Pimenta officinalis*), Cloves (*Eugenia caryophyllata*), Cardamon (*Elettaria Cardamomum*), the Madagascar Clove (*Ravensara aromatica*), etc. The very fine Nutmeg trees are upwards of seventy years old. The spices "nutmeg" and "mace" are respectively the seed and the scarlet netted aril which surrounds the latter. Returning, and crossing through the Rockery, which is occupied chiefly with ferns and shade-loving plants, the glass-roofed CONSERVATORY is reached. This contains a varied and interesting collection of ornamental plants, including several of the Cactus family, desert plants from South America, etc., which at Peradeniya require protection from the wet climate. Joined by a short corridor is the FERN HOUSE, containing a collection of exotic ferns on one side, and of ornamental pot plants indigenous to Ceylon on the other. Close by are the Curator's Office, Seed houses, Stores, etc.

GIANT CREEPER (*Monstera deliciosa*).

Returning to the carriage drive, observe on the left by the side of the road an interesting collection of Insectivorous or Pitcher plants—species of ***Nepenthes*** (including the only Ceylon one, ***Nepenthes Distillatoria***), and ***Dischidia Rafflesiana***, a small climber from Java, with curious bladder-like leaves. Here also is

Orchid House, Interior.

the striking Mexican creeper (*Monstera deliciosa*), with huge perforated leaves and long cone-like edible fruits. The ORCHID HOUSE may now be visited. Here are principally foreign orchids, including species of *Cattleya*, *Lælia*, *Phalænopsis*, *Vanda*, *Stanhopea*, etc. The principal indigenous species may be seen in the Orchid garden recently formed near the Fernery, which may now be visited by taking the straight path to the right. Quitting the Orchid House, notice on the left-hand side of the path a fine specimen of the Giant Orchid (***Grammatophyllum speciosum***), the largest orchid known, the flowering spikes rise six or seven feet above the crown. Notice especially the beautiful

Giant Orchid (*Grammatophyllum speciosum*).

view obtained across a valley on the right, this part having been recently opened out as an extension to the floricultural section. Leading down to it is the ARISTOLOCHIA PERGOLA, including the curious-flowered *Aristolochia ridicula*, the Goose-flower (*Aristolochia gigantea*, var. *Sturtevantii*), the very pretty-flowered *Aristolochia elegans*, and others. These climbers are popularly known as Fly-catchers, the peculiarly formed flowers acting as a trap for insects, which are usually attracted by a carrion-like odour emitted by the flowers, and are promptly captured and utilised by the plant. Continuing under the bowers and down a flight of steps, the path passes through a collection of ORNAMENTAL CLIMBERS trained in festoons between pillars, among which are many interesting and beautiful species. Proceeding a little further, the PALMYRA AVENUE is seen on the right, the new ROSE GARDEN opposite in front, to the left of which is the ORCHID COLLECTION (now in course of formation), and then the FERNERY immediately on the left. The latter especially should not be missed. This was originally formed in 1861, extended and improved in 1898, and is now prettily laid out with

FLOWER GARDEN.

FERNERY FROM PALMYRA AVENUE.

GIANT ANTHURIUM (*Anthurium Warocqueana.*)

winding paths and small water channels. It is well shaded by lofty trees of "Bulu" (*Terminalia Belerica*), "Nadun" (*Pericopsis Mooniana*), "Galmora" (*Pometia eximia*), "Bead" tree (*Adenanthera pavonina*), whose seeds are used as weights by jewellers and apothecaries, Ceylon oak or "Kon" (*Schleichera trijuga*), "Timbiri" (*Diospyros Embryopteris*), Marking-nuts or "Badulla" tree (*Semecarpus Gardneri*), and others. On the tree trunks many interesting epiphytes and creepers of Aroids, Pandani, Bromeliads and Ferns are growing; the last named include *Lygodium*, *Acrostichum* and *Nephrolepis*. Here may also be seen several varieties of the ornamental but dangerously acrid Dumb Cane (*Dieffenbachia*), a slight touch of the juice of which on the tongue will produce inarticulation or dumbness which may last for several days. Notice in the centre the handsome fern-like climber, "Dada-kehel" (*Raphidophora decursiva*), reaching to a height of over sixty feet.

COCOANUT PALMS (*Experiment Station*).

Leaving the Fernery by the south side, the FLOWER GARDEN is again reached. This was begun in 1895, and is now one of the most attractive features of Peradeniya. In the centre is the OCTAGON CONSERVATORY, accommodating a choice collection of ornamental shade-loving plants, which here luxuriate (see page 12). The ever-green climber growing on the sides and upright portion of the top is the "Water Lemon" (*Passiflora laurifolia*), which does not fruit here. The pyramid-shaped tree on the lawn is the handsome "Tembusi" of Malaya (*Fagræa fragrans*), with sweet-scented flowers. On the opposite side, near the Octagon House, are two noble palms with pendulous feathery leaves *Oncosperma fasciculatum*, or "Katu Kitul," and *Oncosperma filamentosum*). Few palms equal in beauty and gracefulness the *Chrysalidocarpus lutescens* of Mauritius, which is here used with splendid effect for grouping in combination with ornamental foliage plants. The curved walk, which brings the visitor back to the carriage drive, is lined on either side by a border of showy *Caladiums*, *Coleus* and *Cannas*, being edged in front by *Alternanthera*. These make an effective display throughout the greater part of the year.

HANTANE VIEW.

Resuming the carriage drive a young avenue of the curious fan-shaped palm *(Didymosperma distichum)*, planted in 1899, is passed on the left. In the corner, close to the road, is a fine specimen of *Pandanus Leram*, the "Breadfruit" of the Nicobar Islands. The slope extending behind this is the ORCHARD, where are representatives of

FLOOD SCENE.

many tropical fruit trees, including "Rambutan" (*Nephelium lappaceum*), "Santol" (*Sandoricum indicum*), "Nam-nam" (*Cynometra cauliflora*), "Mango" (*Mangifera indica*), "Sapodilla" (*Achras Sapota*), "Coco-plum" (*Chrysobalanus Icaco*), "Avocado-pear" (*Persea gratissima*), "Kamaranga" (*Averrhoa Carambola*).,

PALMYRA AVENUE.

SILK-COTTON SHED FROM *Bombax malabaricum*.

"Cashew-nut" (*Anacardium occidentale*), "Loquat" (*Photinia japonica*), "Pomegranate" (*Punica granatum*), "Anchovy Pear" (*Grias cauliflora*), and others. A young avenue of Coconut palms (*Cocos nucifera*) branches off to the left. The Coconut palm may be said to be the most useful tree of the tropics, furnishing the natives with almost all their requirements; its uses are said to be as numerous as the days in the year. Coconut cultivation in Ceylon forms an industry next in importance to that of Tea. Further on, on the left, is the CANARIUM WALK, which passes a row of "Java Almond" trees (*Canarium commune*) with remarkable buttresses to the stem; the kernel of the fruit is edible and resembles an almond. At the foot of the hill the level RIVER DRIVE is reached. Note on the left some very fine specimens of the South American "Guango" or "Rain Tree" (*Pithecolobium Saman*), introduced in 1851 and now largely used as a shade tree for roads throughout the Island, which purpose it admirably answers; the pods are sweet and eaten by cattle.

Here a very pretty view is obtained down the river, showing Hantane Hill in the background, with Tea plantations along its lower slopes; in the foreground is a clump of the majestic Giant Bamboo (p. 22). Close

OLD OREODOXA AVENUE.

Papaw Tress in Fruit.

to the road on the left is a row of Cannon-ball Trees (*Couroupita guianensis*), so-called from the large woody fruits they bear on the stem. Behind these is a small plantation of Sisal Hemp (*Agave rigida*, var. *Sisalana*), cultivated for the valuable fibre obtained from the thick succulent leaves; also a clump of Sago palms (*Metroxylon Sagu*), the creeping stems of which are the principal source of the sago of commerce. Further back are the NURSERIES, where the propagation of useful and ornamental plants is carried out on a considerable scale. At the south end of the Nursery are some climbing Pepper plants (*Piper nigrum*), and at the opposite end similar plants (*Piper Cubeba*), whose fruits form the Cubebs used in medicine. Close to these are some Mauritius Hemp plants (*Furcrœa gigantea*), the leaves of which yield a good fibre. Close to the road on the right is a Rose Apple tree (*Eugenia malaccensis*), and further on, on the left, is the Ceylon Iron-wood or "Na-gaha" (*Mesua ferrea*), an ornamental

Vanilla Cultivation.

tree with large white and scented flowers. Proceeding, the PALMYRA AVENUE (*Borassus flabelliformis*), now eighteen years old, is passed on the left. The Palmyra palm is largely cultivated in the drier climate of the north of Ceylon, where it almost rivals the Coconut palm in its numerous uses to man; the fan-shaped leaves, like those of the Talipot palm, are made into "ola," which is largely used as paper by the natives of North Ceylon and South India for the transcription of native texts. To the right of the avenue is a VEGETABLE GARDEN, where the collection and improvement of tropical vegetables, and the acclimatisation of exotic ones, are carried on. Yams, Arrowroot, Cassava or Tapioca, Sweet-potatoes, Pineapples, Snake-gourds, etc., may be seen here. Here also is a small plantation of Camphor trees (*Cinnamomum Camphora*), which thrive better at a higher elevation. Camphor is obtained by distillation of the wood and leaves, being afterwards submitted to a process of sublimation. Next to these

FLYING FOXES AT REST.

FLYING FOXES ON THE WING.

are some allied trees (*Cinnamomum Cassia*), whose strongly aromatic bark affords "Cassia Bark" or "Cassia Lignea," used for similar purposes to Cinnamon. Further on are several trees of the Mangosteen (*Garcinia Mangostana*), the fruit of which ranks amongst the most delicious of tropical fruits. On the river side of the Drive is noticeable the Red Cotton-tree or "Katu-imbul" (*Bombax malabaricum*), which is completely deciduous; it is a striking object in January and February when bare of leaves but covered with large, fleshy scarlet flowers, the calyces of which are edible. On the approach of rainy weather in April the cotton pods burst open and

ARECANUT PALMS.

fill the air with their flaky white contents, suggesting a snow storm. The road now enters the old avenue of *Oreodoxa regia*, the Royal Palm of Cuba, planted about fifty years ago, and now rapidly decaying.* On the left

GIANT BAMBOO, CLOSE VIEW.

*This has now been interplanted with an avenue of *Oreodoxa oleracea* or Cabbage Palm, a taller and more effective species for this purpose.

is the EXPERIMENT GROUND, where various important economic plants are grown in small plots; these include varieties of Cocoa or Chocolate-tree (*Theobroma*), Coffee (*Coffea*), Rhea or Ramie (*Bœhmeria*), Cardamoms (*Elettaria*), Plantains or Bananas (*Musa*), Bowstring Hemp (*Sanseviera*), Mulberry (*Morus*), Sugar-cane (*Saccharum*), Vanilla (*Vanilla Planifolia*), also "Coco" or Cocaine plant (*Erythroxylon Coca*), the leaves of which furnish cocaine and are largely used as a stimulative masticatory in South America. On the river bank are several trees of the semi-naturalised Paper Mulberry (*Broussonetia appyrifera*), the inner bark of which is manufactured into paper in China and Japan, and into "tapa cloth" in the South Sea Islands. Here also are cultivated the two useful fodder grasses—Guinea-grass (*Panicum maximum*) and Mauritius or Water-grass (*Panicum molle*). Coming to the end of the palms, the visitor passes on the left the young BROWNEA AVENUE (*Brownea grandiceps*) planted in 1900, and interplanted with *Cassia multijuga* in 1904. Both these are natives of Tropical America, and few trees can surpass their beauty when in flower.

SCREW PINE.

JUNGLE SCENE.

Mowing the Sensitive Plant.

The drive now enters the ARBORETUM, passing between two magnificent clumps of the Giant Bamboo (*Dendrocalamus giganteus*). An object of much interest usually visible on the river bank here is the colony of large bats or Flying Foxes (*Pteropus Edwardsii*). These fruit-eating animals roam at night in search of food, and congregate during the day in enormous numbers in the tops of lofty trees, always suspended with their heads downwards. Further on a pretty vista across the Arboretum is passed on the left. This part of the Garden is now being gradually arranged according to families and Natural Orders, the east side being occupied chiefly by *Gamopetalæ*, and the opposite by *Polypetalæ*. Paths traverse the interior, rendering all parts accessible. Some few yards from the road may be seen a fine clump of Arecanut palms (*Areca Catechu*), with remarkable straight stems of uniform thickness (p. 22). On the river bank are some Candle Nut trees (*Aleurites triloba*), the seeds of which are a valuable source of illuminating oil to the natives. Continuing, the North Drive is passed on the left. Notice in the corner some Kananga or "Ilang-Ilang" trees (*Cananga odorata*), whose flowers yield the well-known Ilang-ilang scent. Behind is the Custard Apple order (*Anonaceæ*), including the "Calabash Nutmeg" (*Monodora Myristica*), Bullock's Heart (*Anona reticulata*), and others. A little beyond, on the right, is the ferry path to the Experiment Station

Bridge View.

WEST RIVER DRIVE.

(acquired by the Botanic Gardens Department in 1902), where different economic plants are grown for the purpose of determining their suitability to the climate, the best modes of cultivating them, and the most profitable way of marketing their products.

The extreme north end of the Garden is now reached, and the drive turns round the western side, following for a considerable distance the river Mahaweli-ganga (Great sandy river), which forms the boundary of the Garden, except on the south side; it is the largest river in Ceylon. The vegetation in this portion of the grounds is being reserved, and left to Nature to form a natural jungle. Many forms of self-sown plant life are already here vieing with each other for the possession of space, and vines, lianas and creepers (chiefly of the natural orders *Menispermaceæ, Ampelideæ, Apocynaceæ, and Leguminoseæ*) form tangled festoons and strangely twisted ropes from tree to tree. Under these the curious Sensitive Plant (*Mimosa pudica*),

JUNGLE ROPES (*Anodendron paniculatum*).

introduced from South America and now a pest in Ceylon, forms a dense covering until killed out by more rampant growths. The short forked road on the left leads to the new Oreodoxa avenue (p. 19), passing on the right a small plantation of Clove trees (p. 13). Cloves are the unexpanded flower buds, dried and browned in the sun. At the summit of the road a pretty view is obtained along the Hantane Vista. Resuming the River Drive for a short distance, the beautiful BRIDGE VIEW comes in sight on the right, showing a fine stretch of the river with the one-spanned Satinwood Bridge (now being replaced by a handsome stone and iron structure), and distant hills beyond. Close to the road is the "Down-tree" or "Cork-wood" of Jamaica (*Ochroma Lagopus*), whose curious cone-like fruit, when expanded and surrounded by its brown downy wool, resembles more a fox's tail than a hare's foot as indicated by the specific name. Further on is a row of Durian trees (***Durio zibethinus***); the large prickly fruit, produced in August and September, is, once its repulsive odour is overcome, esteemed by many as one of the finest fruits in the world. Presently the short WEST ROAD is reached, up which the visitor should turn. Notice here the immense tree of "Nuga" (***Ficus** laccifera*), a kind of Banyan, stretching across the road and forming a gallery of stems, which originate as aerial roots, some of which are thrown down at great heights from the

GREAT CIRCLE.

THWAITES MEMORIAL.

branches; when they reach the ground they increase rapidly and form stout columns. Close to the West Road, on the right, is a "Mee" tree (*Bassia longifolia*), which yields a valuable oil from the seed, used for medicinal and culinary purposes.

Arriving at the GREAT CIRCLE—a flat lawn nearly four acres in extent, with a handsome group of palms in the centre—the drive to the left should be taken and followed for three-quarters of the Circle. The young avenue of Royal Palms (*Oreodoxa regia*), planted in 1898, is presently passed on the left, and through it a fine vista is presented. On the knoll close by is a seat under the shade of a "Sapu" tree, from which some striking views are obtained. On the left, Section D on the map, are numerous objects of botanical interest, chiefly of the Natural Orders *Sterculiaceæ*, *Celastraceæ*, *Sapindaceæ*, and *Dipterocarpaceæ*. Here are some specimens of the gigantic climber *Anodendron paniculatum*, or "Dul" of the Sinhalese. Round the Circle are some of the most beautiful trees of the tropics, including the scarlet-flowered *Spathodea campanulata* of tropical Africa, and several which have been planted by distinguished Royal visitors. The first of these arrived at is a young

MOWING THE GREAT LAWN.

tree of the gorgeous-flowered "Flamboyante" of Madagascar (*Poinciana regia*), planted by Princess Henry of Prussia in 1899; then a "Bo" or "Peepul" tree (*Ficus religiosa*), planted in 1875 by our present King; and some distance behind, a West African Breadfruit tree (*Treculia africana*), planted in 1903 in commemoration of His Majesty's Coronation. The "Bo" tree is intensely sacred to the Buddhists, being always planted near their temples. Their religion forbids the cutting of a branch or uprooting of a seedling of this tree, regardless of position or locality. A "Bo" tree at Anuradhapura, the ancient capital of Ceylon, now an interesting city in ruins, is the oldest

LABORATORY, HERBARIUM, LIBRARY, ETC.

LIVE SNAKES ON A TEA BUSH.

historical tree in the world, being planted 288 years before Christ, and is therefore 2,194 years old; it is yearly visited and venerated by thousands of pilgrims. On the crest of the hill overlooking the Circle is the THWAITES MEMORIAL, a small Kandyan building (p. 27), and on the left of the path leading up to

SECTION OF TERMITE'S (OR "WHITE ANT'S") NEST.

it is a young "Na" tree, or Ceylon Ironwood (*Mesua ferrea*), planted in 1891 by the Czar of Russia. Next to this are seen a *Brownea grandiceps* tree, planted by the King of Greece in 1891: *Amherstia nobilis*, planted by Prince Henry of Prussia in 1898; and "Asoka" (*Saraca indica*), planted by the Emperor of Austria in 1893. On the opposite side of the Circle, near the Laboratory, is a small "Cannon-ball" tree (*Couroupita guianensis*), planted by the Prince of Wales in 1901. There also is a splendid example of the *Pterocarpus indicus*, a handsome tree affording valuable timber, used in gun carriages, etc. Coming to the junction of the roads, the visitor should turn into the well-shaded MAIN CENTRAL DRIVE (p. 10).

E. E. GREEN, F.E.S. (GOVERNMENT ENTOMOLOGIST).

At the corner of the road, on the right, is a tree of *Cassia multijuga* (p. 23), which produces its large sprays of beautiful yellow blossom in August and September, and opposite to it a "Muruta" (*Lagerstrœmia Flos-reginæ*), meriting its name by its elegant masses

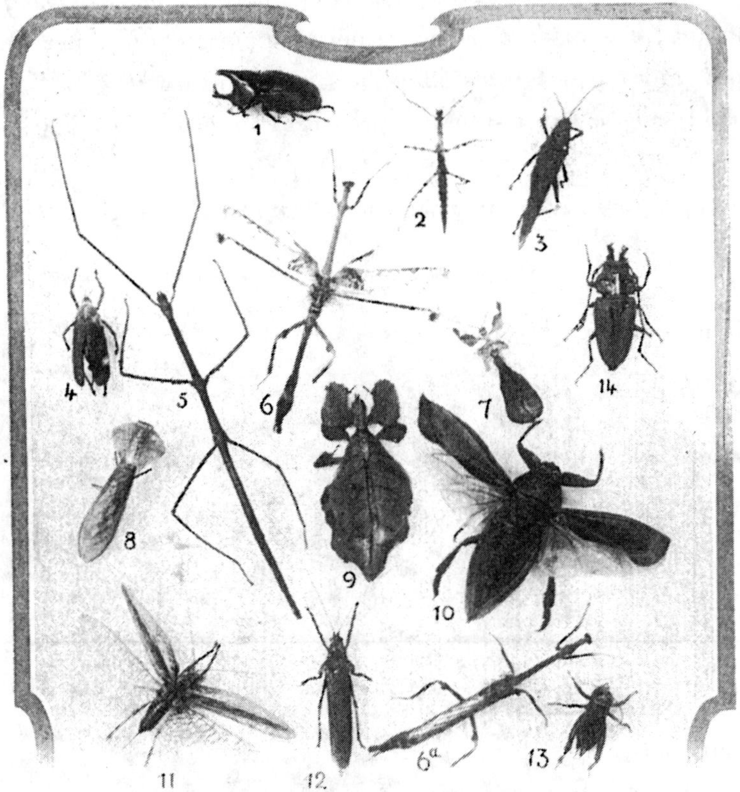

Some Queer Insects of Ceylon.

1. Rhinoceros Beetle. 2. Thorny Stick Insect. 3, 4, 11, 12. Locusts. 5. Bamboo Stick Insect. 6, 6a. Stick-like Mantis, with expanded and closed wings. 7. Leaf Insect (male). 9. Leaf Insect (female). 8. Cobra Mantis. 10. Giant Water-bug. 13. Cricket. 14. Beetle.

of mauve flowers. On the right-hand side may also be seen the Nux-vomica tree (*Strychnos Nux-vomica*), whose very poisonous flat seeds afford strychnine and nux-vomica, both poisons valuable as tonics and heart stimulants. On the left is a tree of the beautiful *Saraca declinata* of Java which produces immense heads of orange-yellow blossom in January and February. The BAT DRIVE turns to the left and leads to the East River Drive, passing on the right the newly-formed Orchid Collection and Rose Garden, also various interesting trees, including the West Indian Necklace tree (*Ormosia dasycarpa*) with curious red and black seeds, which are much prized for making buttons, necklaces and other ornaments; the "Shea Butter" tree of West Tropical Africa (*Butyrospermum Parkii*), from the kernel of which a fat is obtained, called "Shea Butter" and used as butter by the natives; the famous Baobab tree (*Adansonia digitata*), also from Tropical Africa, and others. Returning to the Main Central Drive the visitor should follow the MUSEUM ROAD opposite, passing on the right a magnificent specimen of a Durian tree (p. 26); next to it, stretching far across the road is a gigantic tree of *Ficus Trimeni*, a species of Banyan.

The MUSEUM OF ECONOMIC BOTANY, situated here on a slight elevation and commanding beautiful

FERNERY FROM MAIN CENTRAL DRIVE.

views, contains many objects of interest, including a series of several hundred specimens of the principal timbers of Ceylon, also numerous examples of native food-stuffs, drugs, oils, fibres, resins, etc. Especially worthy of notice are the specimens of the true Ceylon Ebony (*Diospyros Ebenum*), the most valuable ebony known, and the rare and much-prized Calamander Wood (*Diospyros Quæsita*), also the handsome Satin Wood (*Chloroxylon Swietenia*). Observe the natural ready-made sack formed from the inner bark of the Sack tree or "Riti" (*Antiaris innoxia*), also specimens of india-rubber and Ceylon lacquer work. On the west side of the building is a small room devoted principally to exhibits of Economic Entomology. Notice the examples of various kinds of Silkworm Moths with their cocoons, the singular Leaf Insects, which closely resemble leaves; the Stick Insects, appearing like leafless twigs; the curious Praying Mantis; the energetic Carpenter Bee and its work; the Leaf Butterflies, which, with closed wings simulate most perfectly a dying or autumn-tinted leaf, even the midrib and veins being represented; also the industrious but destructive White Ants, whose castellated nests are striking objects in the neighbourhood, but are kept in check in the Gardens by being repeatedly dug out. The whole colony of these ants emanates from a single "queen," who is many hundred times larger than the "king" and ordinary workers. In the figure, which shows a medium section of a large nest, the queen may be seen occupying the royal cell (indicated by a small white flag). The sponge-like substance in the larger cavities serve the double purpose of nurseries for the young insects, and for the growth of a fungus upon which they feed. These cavities are also frequently made use of as breeding ground by snakes.

CANDLE TREE.

Mr. Green, the Government Entomologist, possesses a critical knowledge of Ceylon insects. His book on the Ceylon *Coccidæ* is a valuable standard work.

Behind the Museum are the HERBARIUM and LIBRARY, also the Offices of the Director, Entomologist and Mycologist. On the right-hand side, lower down, is the LABORATORY for general scientific research, built in 1900. The Library, which is extensive and up-to-date, contains a large series of coloured drawings of Ceylon plants, also busts of the famous Charles Darwin and Sir William Hooker,

"Double Coconut Palm" or "Coco-de-Mer."

the latter being the first Director of Kew Gardens, London, the head-quarters of British botanic gardens. Carriages may regain the Main Central Drive and continue as far as the Monument Road. In passing the Fernery, on the left, a very pretty vista is obtained through this and the Palmyra Avenue, both already noticed. The GREAT LAWN, park-like in appearance and beauty, is presently seen through an opening on the right. The BORDERS which line the drive on both sides contain a large variety of tropical plants which are of considerable horticultural or botanical importance. In the corner, on the left, is the Benzoin tree of Sumatra (*Styrax Benzoin*), which affords the fragrant gum-resin known as "Benzoin," used largely in incense and to some extent in medicine; further on is a Teak tree (*Tectona grandis*), whose timber is unsurpassed for durability and general usefulness, and close to it the "Divi-divi" (*Cæsalpinia coriaria*), the pods of which are a valuable source of tan. Notice on the right the

Monument View.

beautiful blueflowered and fine foliaged tree, *Jacaranda mimosæfolia*, and further on the curious "Candle" tree (*Parmentiera cereifera*), the pendulous fruits of which are a close imitation of the old-fashioned tallow candles, also the "Ayapana Tea" (*Eupatorium Ayapana*), and the Curry-leaf tree or "Karrapincha" (*Murrya Kœnigii*), whose aromatic leaves are invariably used for flavouring

LAKE AND GIANT BAMBOOS.

curries. Overhanging the road is a handsome Brazilian tree (*Schizolobium excelsum*), which produces its beautiful yellow flowers when completely bare of leaves.

Turning down the MONUMENT ROAD (p. 11), the magnificent Coniferous trees—chiefly the New Zealand "Kauri Pine" (*Agathis robusta*), and the Norfolk Island Pine (*Araucaria Cookii*)—are conspicuous objects. Some distance from the road, on the right, is a young "Souari" or Butter-nut tree (*Caryocar nuciferum*), whose fruit is said to be the most delicious of the nut kind. Further on, close to the road, is the "Mâté" or Paraguay Tea (*Ilex paraguayensis*), largely cultivated

BREAD FRUIT TREE OR "RATA-DEL."

in South America, and used like tea. Opposite, on the left, in the corner, is a "Double Coconut Palm" or "Coco-de-Mer" (*Lodoicea sechellarum*), the large and singular fruits of which were known for a century, found washed up on the shores of the Indian Ocean, before the palm itself was discovered. This specimen, being a male, produces no fruit; it is now fifty-five years old, and has flowered freely for the past fifteen years. The "Double Coconut" is noted for its slow rate of growth, producing but one leaf a year; the nut takes ten years to ripen. On either side of the road are several young plants of this palm, grown from seed sown *in situ* in 1903 and intended to form an avenue in time. The road up to the Monument is shaded on either side by magnificent trees of "Gal-mora" (*Pometia eximia*), "Bulu" (*Terminalia Belerica*), the nuts of which are used in tanning, being known as one of the myrobalans of commerce, and others. The Monument, erected in 1855, commands some fine views in different directions. The carriage drive should be followed to the right (Jonville Drive). Along the edge of the Great Lawn are some trees of "Sapu" or "Champac" (*Michelia Champaca*), whose sweet-scented yellow flowers are commonly used as temple offerings and sometimes for decorating the hair of Tamil

River Scene.

TALIPOT AVENUE.

women. Up the slope on the left is an Indian Cork Tree (*Millingtonia hortensis*) with white sweet-scented flowers, and in the corner on the right is a tree of *Magnolia sphænocarpa*, with large white flowers. The sharp curve to the left should be taken to join the WEST RIVER DRIVE, which is continued for a short distance. Here a striking view is obtained down the river, with Gangaroowa Hill in the distance. On the opposite side of the river, which is a continuation of the Government Experiment Station, cultivated Coconut palms may be seen, and on the river bank the "Mauritius" and "Guinea" fodder grasses (p. 23). In the ROCKERY BANK on the left is an interesting collection of succulent plants, *Aloe, Agave, Bromelia, Euphorbia, Opuntia, Pitcairnea*, etc. Notice on the right a fine sheet of the yellow-flowered *Allamanda nereifolia* scrambling over the bank in a naturalised state, and opposite, in the corner, the South American climbing shrub, *Petræa volubilis*, which forms a beautiful spectacle when covered with its copious sprays of violet and turquoise flowers. The drive here leaves the river bank, and, skirting the lake, passes the SOUTH DRIVE, which should now be followed. On the slope towards the Monument are some fine trees of the Australian Silky Oak (*Grevillea robusta*), introduced in 1856, and now largely planted throughout the higher elevations of Ceylon for shade, wind-belts and fuel. The two magnificent clumps of bamboos here will at once attract attention—that on the right is the strong Building Bamboo from Java (*Gigantochloa aspera*), and that on the left the Giant Bamboo of Burma (*Dendrocalamus giganteus*). This latter is the largest bamboo known, and luxuriates at Peradeniya to an extent seldom known in its native country, its culms attaining a height of over 120 feet and a diameter of about 10 inches; these appear during the rains in June and July, and grow at the rate of over a foot in 24 hours. Compare these grasses—for such bamboos really are—with English or European grasses!

In the LAKE may be seen growing straight out of the water the Pith-tree or "Shola" (*Æschynomene aspera*), the light pith-wood of which is used in the manufacture of sun hats; also the Papyrus of the Nile (p. 12), Bulrushes, Water-lilies—including the Giant Water Lily of the Amazon (*Victoria regia*), whose huge tray-like leaves grow several feet across, the flowers being about 10 inches in diameter, and sweet-scented. The HILL WALK is passed on the left, and further on in the hollow a small plantation of Cocoa or Chocolate plants (*Theobroma Cacao*), the seeds of which furnish the cocoa of commerce. Here also are trees of the Panama-rubber (*Castilloa elastica*), the "Arnatto" (*Bixa Orellana*), of which the pulp surrounding the seeds

1. Travellers' Tree. 2. Panama-Hat Plant. 3. Nicobar Bread-Fruit.

SATINWOOD BRIDGE.

affords the dye of this name, the "Chaulmoogra" (*Gynocardia odorata*), yielding an oil from the seeds, much used as a remedy for rheumatism and leprosy. On the other side of the Cocoa is a group of Para Rubber trees of South America (*Hevea brasiliensis*), the source of the most valuable rubber of the present day; the tree was introduced to this country in 1876, and is now largely cultivated in Ceylon and equatorial regions generally. Further on, a striking glimpse of the river is obtained between two more clumps of Giant Bamboos. Close to these are some Sandal Wood trees (*Santalum album*), whose fragrant wood is largely used for carving and various ornamental purposes, as well as for burning as incense in temples.

The noble TALIPOT AVENUE, planted about 1885, is now reached. This, *Corypha umbraculifera*, may be called the chieftain of the palm tribe, attaining, as it does, to greater proportions of leaves and trunk than any other palm known. The immense fan-shaped leaves are at their largest size when the plant is about twelve years old, before it forms a trunk; they measure several feet across, and are largely made into fans, umbrellas, portable tents, etc. Known as "ola leaves," they have been used from time immemorial to the present day for writing native text upon by means of an iron stylus. The large hard seeds are made into buttons and ornaments. When from thirty to fifty years old, the palm produces from the summit an enormous canopy of creamy white inflorescence, followed a year or more later by ripe seed, and shortly after by the death of the palm. Behind the palms, on the right, are different kinds of Gutta-percha trees (*Dichopsis*), and further back along the river bank are the principal rubber trees known, viz., *Hevea*, *Castilloa*, *Manihot* or "Ceara rubber," *Funtumia* or *Kickxia* "Lagos rubber," *Mascarenhasia*, etc. On the left is the HERBACEOUS GROUND, occupied by a large and interesting collection of herbs aud undershrubs, all labelled and arranged according to their families; they include the powerfully narcotic Ganja Plant (*Cannabis sativa*), and many others of medicinal and economic value. Continuing the drive, two small trees of Lignum Vitæ (*Guaiacum officinale*) from the West Indies are passed on the left, close to the road; the extremely hard wood yields a green resin used in medicine. Further on, on the right, is a group of the West African Kola-nut trees (*Cola acuminata*), whose seeds are extensively used as a stimulant and masticatory by the natives of tropical Africa, and at one time took the place of money as a medium of exchange; they are also used for manufacturing medicated wines and ærated beverages. Notice on the left the Bread-fruit tree or "Del" (*Artocarpus incisa*), whose fruits form the staple food of the natives of the South Sea Islands; and are relished by natives of the tropics generally, behind this is the Lovi-lovi tree (*Flacourtia inermis*), with tempting-looking but very sour fruits. The drive here ends in a wide oval loop, enclosing the classified PALM COLLECTION. Taking the lower branch, the BAMBOO COLLECTION is first passed on the right, then the SCREW PINES (*Pandanus*); here a close view of the Bridge is obtained. Next are passed the Traveller's Tree (*Ravenala madagascariensis*), *Aloes*, *Yuccas* and *Cycads*. Further back, along the boundary and public road, are some tall trees of the Beef-wood or "She-oak" (*Casuarina*), which do not bear true leaves, and whose wood is very hard and heavy. Before leaving the palms observe in the corner the two trees of the "Doum Palm" of the Nile (*Hyphæne thebaica*), distinguished amongst palms by its branching habit. Carriages must return by the drive, but visitors should follow on foot the broad HILL WALK, joining the carriage drive at the Lake. Among the trees passed on the right are the true Guttapercha tree (*Dichopsis Gutta*), now almost extinct, the "Ordeal Poison" of Madagascar (*Cerbera Tanghin*), the African "Arrow Poison" (*Acokanthera*

Jak Tree in Fruit.

spectabilis), and the "Mahwa" tree (*Bassia latifolia*), whose fleshy flowers form an important article of food in Central India. On the left, further on, are the Horse Radish tree (*Moringa pterygosperma*), whose roots form a good substitute for horse radish, and whose seeds yield the Oil of Ben; the Mustard Tree of Scripture (*Salvadora persica*); and on the right again, the Quinine or Cinchona Bark (*Cinchona spp.*); the useful Bengal "Kino" tree (*Butea frondosa*), which yields a medicinal resin and oil; the flowers are used for dyeing, a lac is produced on the twigs, and the inner bark yields a good fibre. Close to this are the "Tonquin Bean" tree (*Dipterix odorata*), whose fragrant pods are used in perfumery, and for scenting snuff; the Jamaica Ebony (*Brya Ebenus*), the Yoruga Indigo climber (*Lonchocarpus cyanescens*), and others.

Regaining the Drive, the LAKE ROAD may be continued to the Entrance Gates. Before turning to the right, observe opposite and close to the road, a Jak tree (*Artocarpus integrifolia*), the immense green fruits of which are an important article of food with the natives, and are the largest fruits known, weighing in some cases up to 70 pounds; Jakwood is the timber most generally used in Ceylon for furniture-making. On the same side, further up, are various interesting trees, including the Calabash tree (*Crescentia Cujete*), the Mammee Apple of South America (*Mammea americana*), young specimens of the Lace Bark tree of Jamaica (*Lagetta lintearia*), the inner bark of which much resembles natural lace and is made up into various ornamental lace-like articles; the once famous Upas tree of Java (*Antiaris toxicaria*), and its Ceylon ally, the "Riti" or Sack tree (*Antiaris innoxia*), (p. 31); the Balsam of Tolu (*Toluifera Balsamum*), and the Cajuput Oil tree (*Melaleuca minor*), which furnishes an aromatic oil used in medicine; the natives make tonic infusions from the curious flaky bark. On the right-hand side of the road may be seen the handsome Brazil Nut tree (*Bertholetia excelsa*), the "Chian Turpentine" tree of the Mediterranean (*Pistacia Terebinthicus*), used in medicine and for flavouring beverages.

Coming to the end of this road, the visitor completes the circuit of the Gardens.

H. F. MACMILLAN, F.L.S., F.R.H.S., CURATOR.

INDEX.

Index—*continued.*

Index—*continued.*

Index—*continued.*

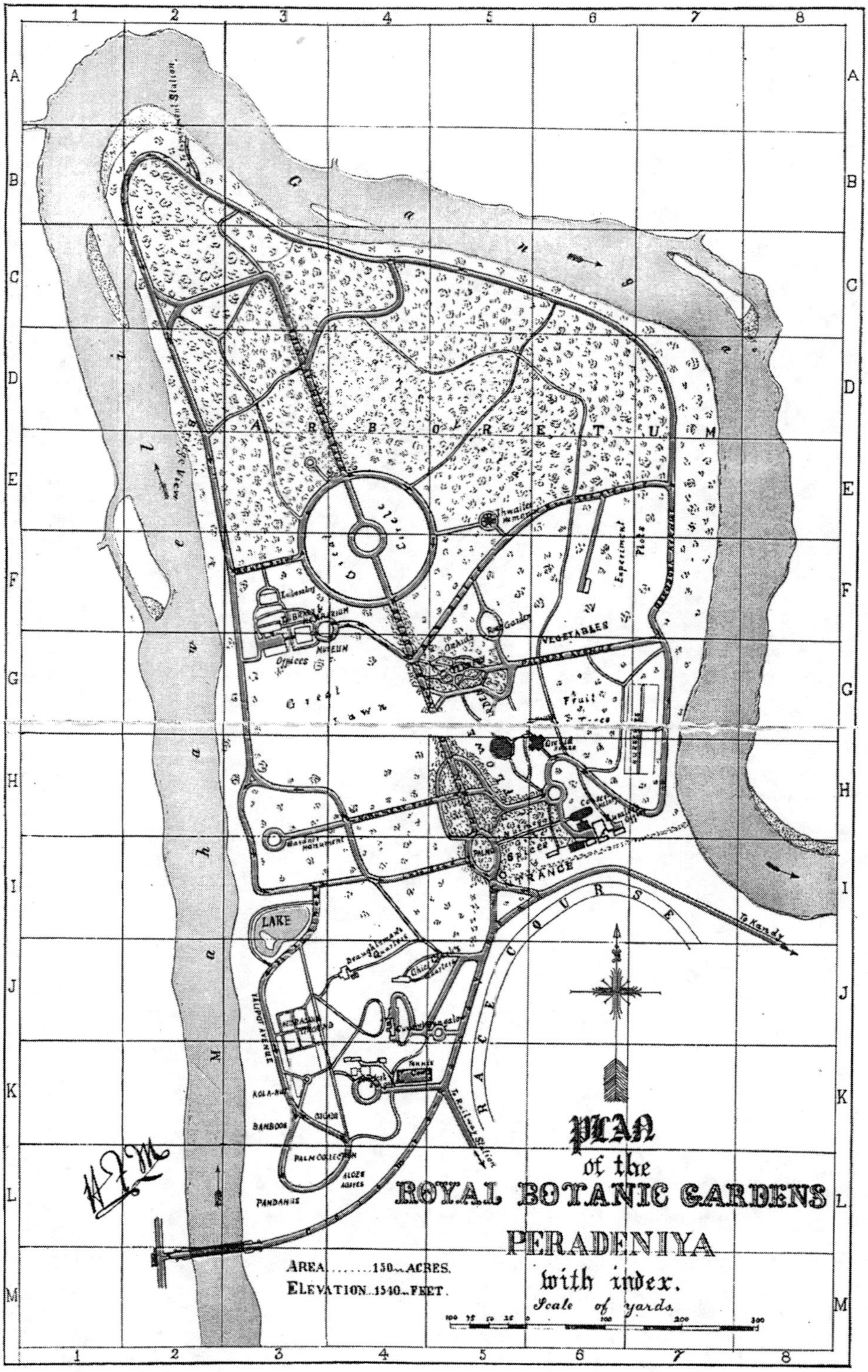
PLAN
of the
ROYAL BOTANIC GARDENS
PERADENIYA
with index.
Scale of yards.
AREA........150...ACRES.
ELEVATION...1540...FEET.
ARBORETUM
Great Circle
Great Lawn
LAKE
VEGETABLES
Experiment Plots
Fruit Trees
Offices
MUSEUM
RACE COURSE
ENTRANCE
To Kandy
TALIPOT AVENUE
PALM COLLECTION
BAMBOOS
PANDANUS
KOLA-NUT
ALOES AGAVES
Bridge View
Mahawelli Ganga